I0517208

BODIES & WORDS

CELIA LISSET ALVAREZ

ASSURE PRESS

An imprint of Assure Press Publishing & Consulting, LLC

www.assurepress.org

ASSURE PRESS

Publisher's Note: Assure Press books may be purchased for educational, business, or sales promotional use. For information please visit the website.

Bodies & Words/ Celia Lisset Alvarez—1st ed.

ISBN-13: 978-1-954573-37-6
eISBN-13: 978-1-954573-38-3

ACKNOWLEDGMENTS

"Climbing the Lighthouse" In *Catamaran* 9.2.

"Coleoptera" In *Blue Mountain Review* Summer 2021.

"Do Please at Least Consider Giving Up" In *Pensive: A Global Journal of Spirituality and the Arts* Spring 2021.

"Going to See Dali" In *Alba* 17.

"How to Make a *Mojito*" In *Blue Mountain Review* June 7, 2021.

"Hunger" In *Prospectus: A Literary Offering* 1 Summer 2012.

"Men" In *Innsae Journal* December 2020.

"Naked" & "Bodies and Words" In *A Collection of Contemporary Love Poems. Special issue*, Adanna Literary Journal.

"Never" & "Maria's Sonnet" In *Iodine Poetry Journal* Spring/Summer 2014.

"Rock Gate Park" & "Florida Honeymoon" In *Poets and Artists* July 2010.

"Seduction" In *Not a Muse*. Edited by Kate Rogers and Viki Holmes. Hong Kong: Haven Books.

"In love there are two things: bodies and words. The words go along with certain bodies, sometimes the name of those bodies, their 'names,' and sometimes the words those bodies exclaim."

— JOYCE CAROL OATES, "WHAT IS THE CONNECTION BETWEEN MEN AND WOMEN?"
(1970)

CONTENTS

BODIES & WORDS

Rock Gate Park
for Agnes

In 1923,
amid the joys of insulin,
treatments for shock, tuberculosis, and scarlet fever,
the desk stapler and the zipper,
when Freud unveiled the powers of the Ego,
Niel Herbert pined the loss of Marian Forrester,
and William Carlos Williams raved over Elsie's filth,
when into the world were born Anthony Hecht,
Aaron Spelling, Norman Mailer, and Bea Arthur,
and Lenin was rendered speechless by a stroke,
Ed Leedskalnin opened the gate of his new home.

For just a dime,
tourists and Floridians alike (some of them his neighbors)
could marvel at the wonders that Ed built,
teasing from the silt the coral rock
the way Zal carved out his son from Roodabeh.
How Ed, at night, by lantern-light,
moved tons of stone all by himself,
his five-foot frame, one hundred pounds, and nothing else,
would puzzle scientists and mystics for years beyond his death.

For Ed had built a home,
not of brick or steel or mortar, but of stone,
and not just walls, but all of it, all of that same
gray coral, porous, amorphous, cold.
Ed built beds, and tables, chairs, and cradles.
Ed built himself a throne, a punishment room, a sundial.
All of these alone, for his bride, his sweet sixteen,
had spurned him, and so he left his Latvian homeland,
left behind the politics and wars,
the reconciliations and expulsions
of Soviets and Germans
to play lumberjack and cowboy

in the last of the Wild West.

How did this tiny cowboy do it, they all ask,
build his own private Stonehenge, his own pyramids?
Did he unveil the secrets of magnetism?
Converse with aliens aboard a spaceship?
Some say he sang the stones to sleep, and lifted them,
a tellurian brand of hypnotism,
tons of coral floating around Florida City
like fossils of the Macy's Day Parade.
Some say it was his own absolutism,
his will to say "Do!" and it be done,
and to this that bride could perhaps stand witness,
if, thirty years after his death,
she had not still refused to visit him.

But I tell you it was love, you fools, love,
irrational, ridiculous, inhuman,
whose root is *no*, and *I*,
an anger reserved only for women,
selfish and relentless and intractable,
demanding and brutal as babies made of coral,
and cradles made of rock: eternal, unyielding love.[1]

---

1. Rock Gate Park is more commonly known as "Coral Castle," close to Homestead, Florida. At 26, Ed Leedskalnin was spurned by his sixteen-year-old bride in his homeland of Latvia, just one day before the wedding. He then moved to Florida City, where he built the enormous castle made of sedimentary rock. No one knows how he was capable of moving tons of rock by himself nor how he was able to construct the castle with such precision and efficacy.

PART I

Climbing the Lighthouse

The tour guide told us
the number of steps:

one hundred twenty-
two. At thirteen, this

meant nothing. All I
could see from the first

step were a boy's calves,
muscled and hairy,

pumping like pistons
up the metal stairs,

each breath mechanic
and full of intent.

Inside the lighthouse
the smooth stucco walls

felt like shells, the salt-
air smell soaked into

the cool white surface.
After fifty steps

my heart felt gripped tight
to my ribcage like

a starfish. There was
no landing to this

circular ascent,

3

just a quick glimpse out

a small window where
I saw blue. My knees

trembled at the top,
but we had made it

all the way, the hairy
boy and I, our pink

faces like mollusks
and the soft-sand beach

still unraveling
far underneath us.

Coleoptera

I remember when we caught that dung beetle
or what we thought was a dung beetle—
those mysterious lessons you used to give me
when I took for granted you were everything:
nuclear scientist, oceanographer, Indiana Jones.
You were only thirteen, but I was nine
and that made you adult in my eyes, capable
of algebra and words like *exoskeleton* you
rattled off like a politician in charge of my own
country. I voted you in and voted you in.
While you were technically no tyrant,
you were master, might as well have worn
a pompadour and stockings and had me
trail behind you with your toilet and tea.

When I saw you kiss her behind your parents'
big crepe myrtle, a revolution took place.
Though I never did make off with your head
I felt my own rolling down the steps that led
to the guillotine of your back porch, your mother's
garden, the soft, black earth of our lost planet
where no plant or beetle, no secret buried bones
would ever be exotic again, or full of promise.

Dragonflies

at some point in the summer
I decided to become a poet
and then that was all
we were still floating in the water
but now   we were like dragonflies
thinking *I'll just rest here a bit*—then
drowned there stiff and pretty
you said to me   *but soft, what light*
through yonder window breaks,
which is all you knew, but—by then   it was
too late   the more you boomed
your tenth-grade sense of me   the more
I wrote about writing   when you
opened up the journal   saw not a word
about you   it was more   than you
were prepared to have found   curses or
jealousies   maybe even love   but still
about you   this language   I had started
speaking   it was more than a possession   it was
some kind of assimilation   some American thing
you asked me   *what will you do?*   and
the words poured out of me   like out of a hole
in the pocket, and I, ever so bad at darning
these needles   all I had between myself and blankness

6

Fashion Report

This season, the girls are wearing
sneakers again, and jeans,
and hooded sweatshirts. They're
smoking again, and wearing their
hair in mean locks over their face.
The lastest fad
is big shirts made of plaid,
and even the prom dresses are
short, tight, red. Red is the color
of the season, blood-red, satin-red.
It's all about the big black bruised eyes,
the pouty red lips. No blush
on the cheeks. The jewelry is chunky,
cheap. The shoes pointy.
The bags are big, bold-colored.
The silhouette boyish, slim.
Thin hips are in. Little tits.
Buckles.

Next season, though,
the flowered dress returns,
with its corsets and its pumps.
In between, the mannequins
will lounge around the windows
with their hinges and their
bald heads and their effortless
fates, until the shopgirls come
and dress them up in beige.

Miss USA Slips and Falls during Miss Universe Pageant

Although she slips only once, CNN shows
Miss USA slipping and falling during
the evening gown competition on a loop,
so that you can see it three times in a row,
and again every 20 minutes or so.
This is the top news story of the day. I
will see it 26 times before I sleep.

Miss USA is praised for her comeback. If
there is such a thing as falling gracefully
on your ass, she has most certainly done so.
Pencil-skirted, one leg goes out from under
her (a slippery sole, no doubt). The other
flamingoes, and she lands, pin-up style, on her
coccyx, the palms of her hands neatly behind
her. Best of all, she gets right back up and smiles,
showing us all that she is capable of
laughing at herself, that she is a good sport,
which no doubt is the reason why she gets fourth
runner-up.

My mother fell on her coccyx
once, off a chair she had been using to reach
a high shelf in the closet. She was in pain
for weeks, and had to take antidepressants.

I wonder what was going through her head right
before she fell, Miss USA's head, that is.
There is so little to have remembered: stand
up straight, smile, don't fall. Perhaps she was chanting
this mantra in her head as she was walking.
Likely falling was her worst fear, and so it
happened. I know what was going on in my
mother's head, because she was screaming how she

8

didn't have enough room in the house and how
she was sick and tired of dealing with it
every single day when she fell. People
normally can walk without falling quite well.
It's when you put the weight of your whole life on
just one foot that it becomes impossible.

Notes on the Semiotics of Whoring

Once upon a time
being a whore was easier.
For one thing,
you knew just what to wear.
A certain shade of red,
a skirt to show the ankle,
the word was out:
love for sale.
Or sex anyway.

Now that respectable women
can easily be found in an electric orange
spandex minidress,
I wonder what the whores must go through.
Here is a woman,
silver pumps, silver purse,
that orange spandex number
I was telling you about.
She is rather heavy,
could have made more stylish choices
to cover up the folds of skin
under her armpits.
She is walking toward the airport,
down LeJeune, at rush hour.
No one pays attention to her.
They honk and hoot at the flower lady,
who is wearing lilac polyester pants
with an elastic waist and an apron
to hold change. Both sets of tits
are equally large, so there is no explanation
for this confusion. Certainly the potential whore
is more attractive, less like mom or
the cafeteria lady, with their nets and coldwaves.
There is a ritzy steakhouse near the corner,

so mystery lady could be waiting for her date,
although one would think she would wait
at the bar if she had any decency.
She could be a tourist
not wise enough to rent a car,
on the way to the hotel
past the steakhouse and the used car lot.

The homeless guy in the pea coat
with the "VETERAN" sign
is getting more business. I myself
have given him two dollars, and he has
blessed me. Yesterday I gave him
one dollar, and he blessed me
just the same. I give him some money
almost every day, but he never seems
to recognize me or my car, ambles
down the line same as always, streaked
with grit. I know he needs my help.

This orange woman, though (her hair
is also orange, ironed into a neat bob
despite the 98% humidity, according to the bank
on the corner, which makes me wonder
what kind of products she uses, and how cheap
they might be, depending on whether she is a whore
or a date or a tourist). Perhaps a sign
would help—"WHORE"—, but might
get her into trouble (there is a police car
right behind me, he's been on my ass
since I left the office). If she is looking for work,
she must be really pissed,
forced to walk a subtle line
in this blunt place.

The Demon inside Me

Her name is Maileidys or something.
She does not fit into these pants.

She craves the figs in the back yard.
She rolls the sugar on her tongue lasciviously.

She locked me in the bathroom.
Bleached my hair near white, staring at me

with her parenthetical eyebrows
set wide as a trap, ready to snap.

She curses at me in Spanish.
Atrévete, comemierda. I let her

buy the red lipstick because I was
afraid she would steal it, otherwise.

She knows I can't walk in high heels.
She stacks them in the closet like daggers.

I tried to exorcise her, but she knows
prayers in both languages. The saints

dote on her melodrama like old women
marking their desperate hours with soap operas.

If only I could name her—she might leave,
but like the Serpent's servants, she is Legion.

Every day she snakes her way
into a new student's smile

into my old grandmother's pain.

12

We must achieve a compromise, I say.

She can have her black lace underwear,
and I can have my blues and grays, my

uniform of neutrals.
Atrévete, comemierda.

Seduction

How could he not find me
exotic? My name stuck to
his tongue like thirst.

I mispronounced myself.
Taught him some new elements:
Rice. Beans. Music. Blood.
*What happens when you mix
them?* he asked, *what happens?*

I grew my hair in long braids.
I could see in the dark.
I could read the future,
holding my fingertips to the air.

I told him stories from the trees
and he translated me,
called me a healer.

At dawn, I flattened out
the sheets, felt the warm
places, like shadows,
where the truest
parts of ourselves had spoken.

Satellite

What bothered you most about him
was that way of his of leaning his face
nose and chin forming a sickle
into anything
a plate of rice
an array of dominoes
a book
your own face
tilted up for a kiss
it was as if
he punctured
hooked
snagged your attention
like a nail through hose
the run gaping like
a smoke ring
until your knee
emerged white
naked
as an ass
this embarrassment
exposure
his constant static electricity
clinging to your dress
and you
nothing but a conduit always
him in the clouds
somewhere the dry ground
in the air lightning
crackling like spider veins
the earth spinning
yet still
always the moon

always the damn moon
anchored in
emptiness

How to Make a *Mojito*

When you said that joke about how many Cubans
it takes to build a raft I thought you were oh so
clever! Clever also that you said it to me.
You showed me how to make souvlaki and I thought
you were so well-traveled! You quoted Marina
Tsvetaeva—*in Russian*—"I know the truth—give
up all other truths!" We read Foucault and though I
could not understand the soul I thought that I had
freed my body and you said that sex is nothing
but a ruse, sex is nothing! Later you made me
show your friends how to make a *mojito* and I
heard myself italicize it. I heard you tell
the joke about how many Cubans it takes to
fill an island and I thought it takes one, just one.

The Internet Answers His Questions

Why don't you write in Spanish?
"Many years / I have fought off your hands, Raza..." So begins acclaimed Chicana poet Gloria Anzaldúa's self-portrait, "Cihuatlyotl, Woman Alone."

Do you have a good black bean recipe?
*No results found for **"Do you have a good black bean recipe?"***

Is that your natural hair color?
I have recently dyed my hair a beautiful, natural looking shade of red. However, I work in a shop, and customers are now constantly asking "Is that your natural hair color?" How can I best respond to this? I don't want to be rude, but this is annoying.

Do you believe in santería?
Do you believe in Santeria/Brujeria? Do you think it works or does it just cause negativity to the person doing it? Does it go back to its origin?

What do you think about the embargo?
What f*cking embargo?

What's a good place to get Cuban food?
Beat The Crowd And Instantly Reserve A Table At 50,000+ Local Restaurants!

Do I have to meet your parents?
I felt my palms grow damp with sweat as I swallowed back the bile rising in my throat.

Why do you wear so much makeup?
It's a professional requirement for my job as a harlot.

Can you translate for me?
These poems don't translate easily.

18

PART II

Going to See Dalí

Driving around St. Pete
wind and rain blurring the neon signs
narrow back street
tiny bump of a hill, curve of the city's thigh,
sending us reeling into space, daredevils
maps and brochures defying their folds
faces gaping at the *Hallucinogenic Toreador*,
our giant pancake breakfast;
we ran with the bulls up the beach
until all the clocks had melted,
and we flared our red umbrella,
victorious over the summer.

Florida Honeymoon

Trapped in that 1950's motel Florida,
there were scarce entertainments when it rained.
One scuffed-up shuffleboard court,
stupid to the elements as the beach,
the rain sopping up the sun-flaked paint
like a paper towel. Sex, of course,
sunburnt to a scorch in the brittle bleached sheets
stamped with the impenetrable codes
of the laundry service on Stickney Point.
Paperbacks wilted on the windowsills,
read to bits, spines cracked and peeling
like our skins. Beer then, cold and sweaty,
six-pack tucked under your arm as you rainwalked
from the corner market, never bringing home
the same food twice: sesame table water crackers,
hot sauce from Peru, Kirin, Corona,
Samuel Adams Cherry Wheat.
Ice creams with hand-printed labels,
fresh peaches 'n cream, pies made
by a woman named Belle, chocolates from Brussels.

We fought over the cigarette lighters.
All day you collected them from between the pillows
and underneath the armchairs, dumped them
on my lap like seashells, vowed to quit
smoking for the last time.

Outside the sun poured into the wet sand,
packed hard gray as cement. I felt it too,
warming my skin, loosening the pores.
By then we'd moved on to wine,
Merlots from Chile, California Chardonnays
in red plastic Solo cups.

22

We sat and watched the sun
drop into a placid silver pool.
At that moment we both felt as if
it would rain again, but not like this.

What Counts

He wants to know what size I am.
How can I explain?
In one store I'm a two, in the other a ten.
If he's in the junior department,
I'm a slash.
If he's in petites, I'm short and fat.
He is overwhelmed with measurements.
He's been waist 34, inseam 32
since he was fifteen years old.
He buys me a blender: three speeds,
hi, medium, lo.
"We can make frozen margaritas," he says,
when I peel off the yards of wrapping paper.
Margaritas, I think:
240 calories,
32 carbs.

Better, My Lover, Dead
after Anne Sexton

How every day I walk in through the gate and read the sign that says
Keep this Gate Closed, and swipe my ID in the clock and think, *there
must be more to living* and how it's been weeks since the last time we
fucked and how it is now that your *blowzy bag* and mine are so very
tired. Baby, I think I'll call you at lunch time, and though I'll look fwd to
it when I finally do it'll be *honey bunch let's go* and I won't remember
what you tell me five minutes after, going down the steps now, heavy bag
full of work that I must balance on my aching shoulders. I'll notice that
sign again, I'll want some *brief bright bridge*, but I'll get back in my car
and it'll be hotter than *a sprouting broom factory*. On the drive I'll think
of coming home and kissing you, some *slow braille touch*—but home is
the dog and peeling away the clothes into the hamper, that bag of work
that I must get to, you with your own bag and your reading glasses, both
of us deep into the night, *each in separate dreams*.

Browsing

Lately I can't seem to find a book I want to buy.
I can tell, just from the cover, all that's about to happen.
Take this one: a black-and-white photograph of a young,
attractive woman in a party dress collapsed on a tile floor.
Trapped by her middle-class upbringing, she has turned
to drugs and alcohol to add drama to her boring life.
By the end of the book, she has undergone therapy,
ditched the drugs, and arrived at the realization
that she doesn't have to live her parents' life
that she can make up her own rules,
paint the dining room bright pink if she wants.
Even so, the martini glasses and Percocet
clink at the edge of her yoga mat every day. She knows
she must never trust herself beyond this moment.

Or take this one: a man on a boat, in silhouette,
on a long silver river snaking to the horizon
just before dawn (or perhaps after sunset, doesn't matter).
He grew up poor and watched his daddy beat his mamma.
Women have been betraying him all his life.
He can only find calm when he fishes this river,
so much like himself: quiet, driven to edges.
This one woman he keeps going back to.
She has children from other men, and he pities them.
Also she is a really good fuck. Finally,
he catches that fish he has been after since he was nine,
that time daddy got so drunk he fell over the edge of the boat,
almost drowned. He lets the fish go,
but never sees the woman again.

You, on the other hand,
have spent more money on books this year
than I have spent on food. You walk around
with a two-foot stack under your armpit, bicep

cut by the spine of the top book.
Everything is interesting to you,
even novelties like *Sharks of the Atlantic*,
Subway Train Poems. When I undress you,
there is a broken capillary in the crook of your elbow,
where you held *The Art of Viking Helmets* too tightly.
You fall asleep with your thumb stuck between the pages
of *Traveling to Nairobi*. All night long I watch the book
rising and falling with your breath, like a ship.
In the morning, your sweat has run the ink, left
a backwards text imprinted between your ribs.

Bodies and Words

The boy and girl in front of me are so attuned to one another
their shoulders look hinged. I've stood in line for an hour
to listen to Joyce Carol Oates, but all I can do
is stare at the back of their heads, slightly tilted towards one another
but not enough to touch. They don't appear to be there yet,
the touching stage, they're pretending now, looking straight ahead
at the tiny author behind the podium but slantwise at each other.
Oates says something subdued and funny, *in love there are two things.*
The girl tilts her head towards him, whispers something in his ear—

It's 1987. My cousin and I are at the movies watching *Dirty Dancing.*
He's been making fun of it the whole time, tossing popcorn at me.
He leans over, whispers in my ear, tickling breath on my neck:
Nobody puts Celia in a corner. The heat
swells up from somewhere near my solar plexus and up around my neck,
pooling around that ear. There's no air, no sound.
Somehow I can see in the dark. We're looking at each other
in a way that cousins do but shouldn't. *In love there are two things.*
He moves away (I can't remember where) and the whole thing
is like it never happened but I can't listen to "Be My Baby" anymore.

The boy and girl get up. He goes one way and she goes another
and all they do is wave. I notice that she's holding hands
with the man on her other side and maybe has been the whole time.
She's not a girl really—maybe mid-twenties—and I think
they must be together because of the way they're holding hands
like all couples do after the fifth year but before the tenth.
I get up too and ask my husband if he's enjoyed the reading. He
says to me, *I couldn't hear a thing, I was watching you the whole time,*
and kisses me on the top of my forehead the way you kiss a child
or a wife of more than ten years. We file out of the bookstore.
It's hot outside and even hotter around my ears. Nobody seems
to have heard Oates say: *in love there are two things—bodies and words.*

28

Just a Little Strange

There was the time I cut off all
my hair, and then the time I wouldn't
cut it at all. When I dyed it black
and when I bleached it white.
Those two weeks when it was blue.

Then there was the time I changed
my name, the month of speaking
in accents, followed by the month
of silence. For a while I knew
French, and Farsi, a little Klingon.

There were the years I tried
to be a poet, a professor, and a wife.
When I wrote sonnets to Kristeva
and baked M=U=F=F=I=N=S.
When I repainted the house.

I also tried not sleeping, lurking
in the dark like a bat, then sleeping
all day long. I tried working
at home. I tried concocting
money-making schemes online.

I tried eating only white food
for a week, dressing only in gray
velour sweatsuits. When I threw
away all my shoes and decided
to go barefoot. That didn't work.

Then there was the time I slit my wrists,
or tried to, at least, didn't write
a note or anything, just tried

to see if you would notice, or stand
there, coming up with more excuses.

Dangerous

Black mold growing in the corners of the shower stall
unread books teetering on the shelf over the bed
termites gnawing behind the baseboards so loud they wake
you up at 4 a.m., ready to fight some battle
to the death against some unseen, indiscernible
evil in the house. Cold beer stacked six-deep in the fridge.
Discarded clothes on the closet floor. Ten pairs of shoes
in the morning before putting those mary janes on.
Dropped calls. Thousand-yard stares. Missed details. This body that
swells like a sponge and just as indiscriminately
soaks up the air into a tight bubble. Loss of sleep.
A thousand hairstyles. Misplaced receipts. Experiments
with eyeshadow. The same answer for every question—
nothing—dismissive, inchoate, inept. Done with it.

Nothing

for Adam Houle

You say you need "the industry of things,"
and it reminds me of Maslow's hammer.
Sorry, but I can't be your shiny nail,
flat and pointy in the right directions.
I'm more the drawer full of rubber bands
refusing to be thrown away even
though there's nothing here that can be bound. I'm
the empty jars of baby food that could
hold anything, if only you knew what.
I'm the shoebox full of those greeting cards
for weird occasions like the death of pets,
the vinyl record collection. Yes, ask
me all you want what you can do for me.
I will always have the same dumb answer.

Never

Let's get to what this fight is really about.
How you and I and the word Never
have lived so long in this house.
There's Never in the little hallway,

its spindly elbow jabbing under your rib.
Never in the kitchen, frying fish.
Never leaves the refrigerator door open
while making a sandwich,

Never burns the toast. Never sticks
the peanut butter knife in the jelly jar.
Never sets the table and forgets the forks.
Never doesn't take out the garbage.

Never doesn't make enough money.
Never cheated on the taxes and got us audited.
Never's in the bathroom, open tubes of paste,
hairy brushes everywhere. Never

leaves the toilet seat up and forgets to put in
a new roll of paper. Never used the last condom.
Never has too many shoes and clothes,
takes up more than half the closet.

Never bought the wrong detergent
that gave you hives. Never's in the yard,
burrowing under the fence. Never gets drunk
at dinner parties and sings showtunes.

Never rides in the car, in the back seat,
screams "this way, that way—watch out!"
You and Never pick me up at work,
complain that I'm late.

Never commands the remote.
Neither you nor I can see our favorite programs.
Never picked the colors of the walls,
which no one likes, and the hideously

striped, lumpy sofa no one sits on.
Oh, Never doesn't do anything right!
Never Never Never Never
Never's in the bedroom, of course,

lying there between us, insomniac,
paranoid, hearing burglars breaking windows,
ghosts playing piano, and gunshots
in the night.

The Etymology of Possums

Scurrying. A temple full of want. Tables set
with scraps. Antelopes of fear, running through a field
dead from snow. Dead branches. Lights flashing, dogs barking.
Whispers and plans, more plans. Listening in the dark.
Sometimes, a high-pitched whine—*electric. What can you
see in the dark?* Myself, myself only. My vast
capacity for ignorance. Underneath our
gardens, tunnels, families—war! Every morning,
evidence of battle. Every night, metronome
sighs pop the silence of this marriage, this life, this
house, this bric-a-brac. As if there could be order.
As if there. More breeding in the attic—breeding,
breeding. Eaves so heavy the skinny pillars bend.
When they snap—all those red eyes, sharpened teeth—appear.

Ditty

The pretty vase that shattered on
the floor—the one that always held
all those flowers that you brought me,
and the cat who knocked it over,

dead at just twelve, and suddenly,
the torn red satin dress, too small
to fit these hips grown wide and soft—
all these tiny losses. Yes, once

I thought my life was over
ruined like a girl knocked up or
a roast left too long in the pot.
How I wept over lost rings, lost

boys, lost keys. Over songs, movies.
Fights and failed tests and clogged up drains.
Trials I would forget in hours, or
many years, but, eventually.

Eventually you get to know
the rhythm of loss like a song
played many times. You learn to hum
along and play the chords by rote.

I've played this tune before. Don't feel
so bad. It's no duet. Our love
is over but—why should I cry?
It's just another thing that's died.

PART III

Hunger

At the red light, behind
a truckfull of men—
versions of denim,
baseball caps pulled down low on the brow,
hunched, muscular shoulders—
I think
what wretchedness, this work,
picking crops for cents on the basket,
dull gray mornings by the fruitstand
waiting to get hired.
Just one day without a job
can mean hunger.

Last Sunday at the swap meet
I gawked at carts and carts of cantaloupes.
Their dimpled, light brown skins
felt like asphalt to my fingers. A woman
in a thick black braid and pocket apron
chose two for me while I watched
a skinny boy chatting up a girl
in tight pink shorts.
¿Que vas a hacer esta noche?

These men now—I count seven—
what fractured selves do they go home to?
I realize I have been staring.
They surprise me, suddenly alive,
grabbing their crotches,
yelling obscenities at me
they think I can't understand.

I'm Easy

You know I'm easy, as eggs over, as pie, as peasy.
A bright smile can knock me up. Like a bowling pin.
Whisper into the back of my ear, and you're in.

You know I'm easy, to catch. As a cold. To please,
as a five-year-old. A quick kiss on the lips is
all it takes for me to conjure up wedding dresses,
bridesmaids, tiered cakes. A plastic couple at the top.

You know I'm easy to keep, like a cat—a litter box,
that's that. Or laminate flooring, a sweep and a mop
and I'm done, a masquerade of solid wood. Knock-knock
to tell if I'm the truth. Which I'm not. You know

I'm easy to lose. Like car keys, like glasses. Taken
for granted. A place for everything and everything
in its place. I refuse to participate. Like paper clips,
earring backs, cigarettes. Palm your pockets for me—
one, two, three. Where did you leave me? Don't forget—

I'm easy.

I Suddenly Like Jazz

My man said admit it, you like jazz. No
amount of denying it would do and
it's true, I thought. The way you can live in
a jazz song—it's not possible in those
pop and punk tunes we used to hear, drumbeat
blindly thumping a rhythm for our bowels.
At least not so easy as sliding down
Billie Holiday's throat like a candy-
coated pill, so fine and mellow. Love is
like a faucet—it turns off and on. Or
maybe like a stereo playing all
our different songs. Sometimes when you heed
an unexpected melody, it makes
you realize how much you have been wrong.

Buddies

He told me fat jokes
with a self-deprecating smile.
Pants so big you can see them
from outer space, he swore.

We read each other poetry like
Victorian lovers, discussing Glück's
penchant for abstract declarations
the dissonance of Plath's consonants,

if poetry and politics should marry.
We watched TV together
commenting on the commercials.
We both wanted to try Giant Cheetos,

see the new *Star Trek* movie.
He was the last person
I talked to before falling asleep,
and the first one I thought of

when I had something to say.
When he asked if he could
come over, I said no. Better
this way, I think. I know how

it would go after a while.
The stories would run out.
The jokes become forced.
We would draw lines between

lyric and language. He would
watch basketball for days, and I
would find someone else I
could pretend to know.

0 – 16

He keeps an imaginary scoreboard
in his head, seductions / rejections.
A block of wood in his brain
full of notches on the wrong end.

And no wonder—flirting his way
into impossible. Not for him
the droopy-mouthed girl who clings
to his every breath like garlic.

Not even the one pretty as a rosebud
about to bloom all over everybody.
No; idiot picks them special,
inaccessible, a classic fear

of success: the best friend's girl,
or the one who's only interested
in homework help. The cheerleader
with the long hair and even longer

legs wrapped around the quarterback.
Girls on television and in movies.
Even married women, too old to listen
to his conversations about comic books

and all his loves gone wrong. What
a moron. What a waste of youth,
of really quite good looks, and a soft
voice. Of a head so full of romance

it hurts to listen to him, like
watching a kitten crossing
a busy street. No wonder it's 0-16.
Or so he thinks, or so he thinks.

Maria's Sonnet

I've thrown out all the old rules.
Bought the patent-leather pumps full price.
Stayed out till 2 a.m. without calling.
Smoked. Drank. Learned to play pool
in tight jeans. Spent all my savings
on a black motorcycle sleek
as a shark, driven it fast
in the rain--helmetless--my hair on end,
sharp as a fin. I've prayed hard
for forgiveness, for temperance,
for sleep, lain awake in the twilight,
making shapes out of shadows.
Making something out of nothing.
Making nothing out of myself.

Your Post-It on My Book of Poems

There they are, your phone numbers,
each time I try to read. I have
three places to call you, cell phone, home,
office—never someplace too far for words.

I read about black trees in a
blacker night.
Branches, empty—the poet
cannot tell the difference. Where
are you now? Eating your peanut butter
sandwiches, your portable foods?
Your name sticks to my gums.
I read of butterflies
trapped in mercury, glass, snow—
someone else's landscape, images
I can neither recognize nor leave behind.

My own phone is nestled in my pocket
like a talisman. Its language of numbers
is clearer than poetry.
It would not hesitate to touch you. Its voice
bridges any distance, quick as thinking.
I am a slower machine. I can feel
the pen's grooves on the paper,
where you carved them, your numbers,
ballpoint, certain.

Contradiction

Pruning metaphors seem apt. Snip something off
to make something stronger, they say. I don't
know anything about plants. I've heard the same
of hair and nails. Trim the ends to make them

grow faster, longer. This has never made sense
to me, the universe's spirit of
contradiction. My inability to
fool it. The universe knows when I want

the damned rhododendron to flower, when I
want to have long hair. If I prune and feed
the plant it withers, and if I spit on it,
call it a whore, it withers. It withers

because it knows. I have cut my hair so short
it feels like velvet, and still it does not
grow, and I have let it live in its own black
miasma of brittle curls, and still it

does not grow. How long have I been trying to
forget you? Shunning every thought that has
you in it? The damned universe—it knows, it
knows. It knows that I don't really mean it.

Heliotropism

Never underestimate the power of attention.
Plants know this.
They say you can talk to plants,
say anything you want, however cruel,
as long as you say it in a sweet and loving tone.
The plant will grow and bloom, will love you.
It is the same with dogs.

Thus when you said those things to me
I felt oxygen coursing through my cells.
I grew and bloomed. I turned to you
like a sunflower to the deadly sun.
The sun is the same.
Indiscriminately warming, heating, burning,
then disappearing, only to return again.
You forget the endless night.
You think the sun is only about you,
there because you wanted it to be,
because you spent the night shivering
and wishing for it. It is the earliest
concept of God: God has heard me,
God has sent this sun for me.

So easy to believe.

In truth the planet is spinning in a void.
The sun is an endlessly repeating
chemical reaction. It is punching
a hole in the ozone layer.
It is melting the icecaps.
It is tanning a girl in California,
growing melanoma on her neck.

Naked

I always thought it was the bra that did it.
That first removal—that first look at the white,
white skin that says to the lover: only you.
After the bra, there's not much left. Decisions
have been made, and all else is haste. The bra is
the border between before and after. And
then, you took off my watch. That watch that had been
on my left wrist since the eighth grade, to which I'd
looked for the school day to end, for morning to
begin, to mark times for medicines and deaths.
Exposed the pink circle of chafed skin even
I had not seen. Ran your warm finger over
the smoothest, most secret part of me. Left me
with no way of knowing when or how to stop.

Scenarios

If the zombies came,
we would have to fight them—
all else would fall away;

perhaps a plague,
some virulent virus—
implacable as a bearded god.

You and I somehow immune,
forced to start over—
for the good of humanity;

some tropical island,
falling coconuts—
that sort of thing;

or a hospital bed;
hairless and emaciated,
I could tell you then.

And die, guiltless as a heroine.
No more trading poetry with each other
as if we were a puzzle. No more

irreproachable seating arrangements
or conspicuously public chit-chats.
We would say,

look, it comes to this—
we have one life to live;
that sort of thing.

Then hellfire, brimstone, damnation—
zombies too numerous to fight

with these crude weapons,

arguments over the right way
to hook a fish or thatch
a palm-frond roof.

Your body worked down to a brown
muscle when I, crackled
by the obstinate sun

speak the death-words
on our bed of ropes,
long before we start to wish

for automatic weapons,
for vaccines, for rescue—
that sort of thing.

PART IV

Peach Summer

All parts of the peach except the fruit pulp and skin are toxic.
These parts contain cyanide-producing substances.

— AGGIE HORTICULTURE

Every day a new crop fell giggling
from the branches, crowding around the roots
in sunset-colored *pamelas*. Breakfast
hummed with their chatter, with their canoe trips,
their bright picnics of cold tongue, their crustless
cucumber sandwiches. There were cobblers
and crumbles, compotes and flans, pies, stewed meats.

Soon we could not bear their threat of decay,
their spots of mold, their sueded, darkening
skin like the bruised hands of old women.
Their stale perfume infused the hothouse nights.
Their gossip became vicious. They complained
of sweats, jealousies and preferences.
Separations were made: tarty, plump, dry.

Finally, our bellies full, we froze them.
We boiled them first, and in our hands they shed
their summer silks like wilting girls. Yellow
juices ran as we cut in, revealing
their blood-red pits. Satisfaction congealed.
We sealed their pulp in bowls, stacked them three-deep
in the freezebin. They wait there still, unthawed.

The Hands Give You Away

My mother says, it's the only part
of the body on which you can't do
plastic surgery. I wonder if this is true;
it must be, since I know there is such a
thing as vaginal reconstruction. So I
slather them with cocoa butter and sleep
in mittens like a storybook cat. Try
being Cuban and keeping your hands
hidden when you talk. Try wearing a
cocktail ring. Try winter. Try doing the
dishes in rubber gloves. Try cleaning the
shower doors with Comet. Try having
absurdly long nails and wearing absurdly
thin hose. Try clothes that have no pockets.
Try nailpolish and a keyboard job.
Remember the days of rotary phones,
the pencil you used to dial. Try texting
someone now. Try opening a can of Diet
Coke. Try anything, anything at all.

Hagheart

She's telling the old guy with streaked white hair
some story about what it was like to study
at the polytechnic in Havana while she buffs
his nails, sitting in front of the giant flatscreen TV
the new management put in about six months ago.

There's been a live concert DVD stuck in there
for at least two months. Same two singers in an
impassioned duet, some guy who is not Antonio
Banderas and some blond who appears on stage
as a surprise, I think.

          I don't come here too often—
try to space it out for at least a couple weeks.
Can't stand the faux white marble tiles and the
frost-tipped women. But I went gray when I was
thirty, the hag inside me pushing out by the roots,
unable to wait even a decade longer. She was always
there, I think, brewing soothing tea and wearing
fuzzy slippers. Finally she had enough. I hate

how his eyes drift up to the line of silver at my crown,
the days when the scan is silent. When he says
you look great today the hag is beat, cowering
somewhere in my solar plexus. So I come here.
Write this poem. Creep out the natives of this land
I don't belong in. They are an efficient hive.

It takes a team sometimes, and I am splayed on a
slab like a roast pig, one frost-tipped woman plucking
at the hag over my eyes while another digs for her
under my nails and a third files down my heels
where her slippers have caused calluses. When they are
done, they hold the apple to my lips, and I bite down.

Memo to My Lover about How I Must Quit Drinking

I write to tell you I have to give up
drinking. The doctor says triglycerides
are marching through my veins like termites, my

heart collapsing like some badly pitched tent.
I think a lot about my heart these days
in metaphors that fail to help me feel

the slimy baby's fist it surely is.
I have given up so much for this heart.
No matter; surely this body is more

than just a well into which I throw my
copper pennies, listening for the sound
of a splash somewhere below my navel,

some cold dark pool of mercurial faith.
Surely that red wine glass on the table
is no more than the cigarettes that crept

into my mother, worming into her
lung, or any of the countless choices
we make daily about colors to wear,

people to love. I could have given you
up just as easily, if the doctor
had said as much. "Here, the lung, you see? that

cloudiness; his hair, when his head rests on
your chest." But doctor, I would say, how much
must I give up? "Begin by allowing

this tenderness no more than ten minutes

every night. One pack a day, one glass
of wine. Soon you'll find you're able to do

without entirely, the body fed
by its own self in perpetuity—
a machine so perfect it feels nothing."

The New Wife

Who could fail to love her darkly shaded eyes?
Her spoon-shaped soul? Her every minute?
even at my thinnest, my thinness
was a knife. It's always the new wives
who bear the son, who sit the throne,
pointy-nailed and glossy, perpetual brides.
The photographer tilts his camera, pries
her tiny buttons, his for one moment alone,
and then another man's for life. What sadness
he must endure, to know such splendors
only fleetingly, the coven of flower girls
draped in butter tafetta, already flaccid
at the curls. Such fair maidens,
they stand around like weeds, like daisies.

Piccata

She pounds the aliform breasts
between square slips of wax paper
beating them with a rolling pin
until they are flat and thin.
She has three plates before her:
flour, egg, and breadcrumbs.
She dips the chicken in each plate,
shakes it out the way some women
will shake out their hair
after a long day. She is not pretty.
She eyeballs the oil in the pan,
waits until it's hot enough for a sizzle.
Cooks each breaded slab individually,
watching the corners for the golden blush,
flipping them carefully.
In the oven, she has some apple crisp,
and on the stove, creamed potatoes.

He is not home yet. This is a ritual:
chicken on Fridays. Although he prefers
roasted, she is gambling on her knowledge
of him, on her ability to tempt. The house
smells of butter, of apples, of herbs and lemon.
When she calls him to the table, he ambles in,
older than she is by many years, and stooped.
He surveys the table. A smile flickers on his lips.
They sit side by side, looking out the window
to the garden she also tends. She cups his chin
in her palm and he says nothing.
As she washes the dishes, she remembers
being young. It was so difficult, to juggle
all those recipes, all that want.
So much uncertainty. Love has an inertia

it must build over the years to keep it going.
Motion to motion, rest to rest.

Then

Whether or not I loved you
is not up to debate.
Loved you I did,
from your curly brown hair
to your cherry red car.
Thirty years later,
though we are still nothing
but friends,
a text from you makes me smile.
I play around
with the idea of telling you.
But I know it would embarrass
you into silence
to hear I still get a pang
of jealousy when you talk
about your wife.
It's not that I want you
to love me now.
I just want you
to regret not having
loved me then.

Company Party

He searches, but the room is full of people,
people dressed in black and pinstripes.
Pinstripes too thin to notice unless you stare,
stare like some kind of lunatic likely to—
to kill you or something in the parking lot,
parking lot full of cars that all look the same;

same people, same cars, and she is not there,
there to tell him a joke that he can laugh at,
laugh at the way she always deflates everyone,
everyone bent on making a good impression,
impressing the bosses or the families of the bosses,
bosses too drunk to care or even notice whether,

whether who knows what? Someone has shown up,
shown up to the dance and danced. But she,
she has this way of wearing a bright red dress,
dress that she is not supposed to wear here,
here where everybody loves her precisely,
precisely because she does not follow the rules,

rules like have just one drink or one date,
date that you brought to show that you're serious,
serious about having a family and not likely to—
to what? To corner the woman in the red dress,
dress that he wants to hike up over her hips,
hips that are round and soft and he can push,

push up against the desk or the wall or whatever,
whatever can get him through this party he—
he just doesn't belong in, he who told his parents
(parents he now takes care of) to fuck off,
fuck off and leave him alone, he who skipped out
out of all those practical classes like math and shop,

62

shopping instead for pot and a little wine and writing,
writing stories and poems and whole novels,
novels that stayed in his head but they were good,
good. She said they were good and she loved,
loved the way he was so creative and moody,
moody but not like the others—sensitive, yes,

yes to his caresses and yes to his proposal and yes,
yes to the first child and the first car and the house,
house that cost him the trip to Prague his parents
(parents who were once wealthy and really,
really did love him) were going to pay for if—
if he straightened up his act and left that girl,

girl who was no longer a girl but a mother,
mother and wife. And what the hell, he thought,
thought that he would be different, that there—
there's no rule that says we all have to make mistakes,
mistakes he knew well from watching his parents
(parents who were once people too, with dreams,

dreams like playing the cello for his mother and—
and what was it? His father had once wanted . . .
wanted to scuba dive or something) who argued,
argued even when they were quiet and busy,
busy doing the dishes and sighing, or reading,
reading the newspaper or one of those mysteries,

mysteries his father kept piling up next to the bed,
bed he never slept in since his back was so bad,
so bad he used to sleep on the floor in the kitchen,
kitchen his mother mopped twice a day because,
because, she said, you have to. So he did it,
did it the first time under the proverbial bleachers,

bleachers so small he was sure the whole world,
the whole world he never really understood,

understood the way you understand how to push—
push a button or a woman, for example, to make it,
make it work, yes, but not the way you understand,
understand say the exact way some people—

people with more brains, maybe—understand,
understand everything like how televisions work,
work in general, for that matter. Anyway he felt—
felt the whole world had seen him do it to this girl,
girl he didn't really love but only wanted,
wanted like he wants this woman now in the red dress.

Tomorrow

You will remember me when you grow old, I know.
Not in between—there will be years when you don't think of me.
There will be years when, every morning, your first thoughts
will be of work, and getting there, the traffic barriers, trips
to airports and hotels. In other years you will dream
of women with long, brown hair, and nights you shared.

You will marry one of these—not the prettiest, but the most quiet,
the one on whom you can project your thoughts. She will be
the mother of your children. She will buy your cereal,
and attempt to read your books (as I did, although you will not
remember this, not yet). You will drop her off at work sometimes,
once the children are in school, and love the way her hips sway

as she walks away from you, and smile. You will get home
one night and fall asleep on the couch and the car will not work
the morning after. One day you will realize you have grown fat.
When you reach over to her white shoulder she will shrug off
your hand, absorbed in a book you have not read and, quite frankly,
disdain. You will hear her sigh as she turns the page. You will

pick up the remote and watch the game. You will not recognize
the salmon walls and dark wood furniture, your aged face
in the mirror. You will check in on your children and find them
asleep, oblivious to you. You will wake up in the morning
and go to work, and your heart will leap into your throat
at the sight of the new girl, brown-haired, bright-eyed. She

always compliments your tie. Asks for your advice. Listens,
lips slightly parted, to every word you say, and you say many—
you tell her about your broken car, and your salmon walls,
you hint at your sad wife. At night, while your wife reads
another novel, pink softcover, you think of the new girl,
put the remote away, grab a book, grab another book. You'll think

you have gone mad—you're not that sort of man. And what
does she know, this stupid girl, the cloying scent of high school
still reeking on her breath like too-sweet wine. You will remember
me then. The way I'd bite my lips and look away. At first you'll
think of your own pain, those brief months so full of longing
when you thought yourself doomed to love me. How wretched

you were, so young, so virgin. How patient I was, to listen
to your babbling, to bear your constant presence, your inept
compliments about my hair, my clothes. If only I had known—
as you (you see it now) how late it is. Tomorrow, if the car starts,
you must shut the door to the office. You must pretend to be
very busy. You must keep your distance. Soon it will be all over.

She will disappear, some school, some job, some guy, some life.
You will be able to eat, to sleep, to breathe. But you
will not be free. Never again. Trust me.

66

Honeymoon Picture

Nothing has really survived but this.
We take the usual pose,
his arm over my shoulder,
my arm around his waist.

But this is not the same
as those other poses, after.
Something's off—
it's not what you'd call youth;

it's a good picture, too.
We are surrounded by the rocks
and tiki torches of our Hawaiian honeymoon.
Whatever kind stranger interrupted

his own pleasures to do us this one favor
had an eye for detail, captured the gloss
of the hibiscus, edged out
the undecorated darkness.

But its unusual nature is not in its background—
it might be those vivid Kodak colors,
a smoothness to our skin, dark hair and lips,
shiny belt buckle, plush green turf—

no, it's not what you'd call youth,
not the clean, bright teeth, or even something
about the tilt of my head that might betray
a foreknowledge of that night's brevity;

not his soldier's posture, as if
waiting to be drilled, or the fingertips
dug into my arm to bring me near;
it's not what you'd call youth—

67

it might be that air of stock photography,
bride, groom, tropical honeymoon,
happily ever after, captured.
Our roles defined by light and shadow.

It's not what you'd call youth, no;
could we but afford the plane fare,
find that old hotel, another couple
would be holding still, standing there.

Jocasta

It seemed like such a good match, Laius.
You and I, and all of Thebes before us.

So dashing you were—even the rape
of Chrysippus seemed something we

could forget. I believed you when you said
you loved me, you could love me. So many

fates were tied to ours—how could we fail?
Every time my blood flowed a river

ran dry. Every time my tears fell
there was drought. Your caresses

were so full of intent—your brow
furrowed, concentrating all your being

not on loving me but on succeeding
in your role as king. Long before the seers,

I knew that we were doomed. Knew
that I could not love your eyes on me,

cold as a soldier's, my body nothing
but a battlefield to prove your sword.

Many times I swore I'd never again touch
you, yet I could not forget the purpose

of my life. Even the eyes of slaves
seemed to glisten with desire, to arouse

in me a longing to fulfill my promise

to this world. How could I not tempt

you? Seduce you? It was only you I
wanted. The rest of the story is nothing

but fantasy. The son whose presence
cannot last. Your death at his hands,

which were your hands when we met.
My freedom from your coldness,

the contest to possess me that leaves me
blameless when I take a strong young boy

into my bed. For a while, I am a woman
again. Effortlessly, children come from us

like sighs. Even when I know—I *know*—
the monster I've become, even then I can

still long for his bright eyes and my bright
reflection in them. It makes perfect sense,

you see, that he and no other could take
your place. Those eyes are your eyes,

restored to wanting me. It is you
that I was after, all along—

he must have known.

Do Please at Least Consider Giving Up
for Rosa and Leonardo

Even now, even as your fingertips
crawl closer and closer to the
fine gray hairs on my wrist, as
your animal static brings my
old-fashioned wind-up watch to
a trembling stop, even now
it is not too late.

When we first noticed
that the breadcrumbs led to nowhere,
that, in fact, we had got into the habit
of wolfishness ourselves,
we had the chance then.
Then we could have said:
"Ah, love, let us be true."
But now, now the books
are packed up on a shelf we cannot reach.

No, my love, let us relent.
Let us pay this check and go,
let the credits roll. Let us
spare ourselves the indignity of passion
at this late a stage, the blushing
wrinkles, the creaking knees
and calloused elbows. Let us go,
straightbacked as we can manage,
down the widest corridor, your token
palm on the small of my small back.
Let us go, content still to be
tailored and respectable old characters,
he who worked hard and she who
loved well. Let us go, and wrap ourselves

in blankets made of wool, and
wait for snow. Let us go.

Watching Rosa

She is going to fall on me, he says,
and doesn't mean it in any cartoonish way,
although he holds her elbow when they walk—
when they used to walk—rather than
disenchant her about her unstable choice of shoes.
Certainly no woman past eighty should be wearing pumps,
no matter how square-healed. No, what he means is
on my watch, she's going to fall. It's an expression of
ownership I would normally bristle at, as if his wife
is no more than his child, as if her falling would be
his responsibility, his fault, his lack of watchfulness, of care,
which it would be, her mind not being what it once was,
although perhaps she's been the sort of woman her whole life
to make unreasonable footwear choices. A foolish woman.

This is his greatest fear on his deathbed, that,
disconnected from his ninety-year-old grip, she will fall.
He also talks about those long hours of work at the bottle factory
where they first met. It was *work*, he says, *work*, and *we were grateful*.
No one fell back then, although he looked after her the same,
gave up his seat on the bus to her, humored and petted her,
and she adored him for it, for more than sixty years.

Now that he is dead no one watches her, of course,
and she hasn't stumbled even once, although she still
insists on those same flimsy heels, and she is humored
by her daughter and the nurses. *She is adjusting remarkably well*,
the daughter says. Surely when she dies her shoes will go
to some charity, and she will lie again next to her husband,
grave to grave, one final pair of dark gray pumps resting
comfortably on cream satin. Grandchildren will gather round,
remembering them both. They will never know
how to keep anyone from falling.

FW: From a Friend

She sends me e-mail warnings about
toxic plants found in all homes.
The hidden germs in queso fresco.
The latest trends in assaults on women:
if someone hits the back of your car,
keep driving.

She says to pass these warnings on
to all my women friends.
She does not seem to think
my men friends keep plants
or eat foreign cheese.
Would hijackers
hit the back of a man's car?

She also sends me
uplifting messages about
how to see the beauty in
my gray hair
(it means I've lived)
my sagging breasts
(it means I've fed a child)
my swollen feet
(it means I've walked).

She sends me
chain letters.
If I pass them on
to five other women
in the next 24 hours,
I could
receive an inheritance
meet the love of my life
get a promotion

74

relieve my lower back pain.

The e-mails have tails
long as litanies,
automatic signatures
brief comments
from all the women
these messages have gone through:
Pat from Melbourne (XOXO)
Linda from Albuquerque (Regional Manager)
Fatima @ gmail.com (love ya).

Sometimes I pass these on.
Dear So-and-So,
do you
have this spiky plant?
need to take this vitamin?
recognize this woman,
killed by a stray bullet
while driving at night
through a strange neighborhood?

Men

I never learned to fear them.
Perhaps I should have.
But they were easy to avoid,
those early, absent fathers,
rainmakers. Love was a dry matter:
stay indoors, watch the sky
for signs of storms.

Once a little grown,
they were theoretical as clouds.
All my comforts and my punishments,
all my justices, were women.
The boys were lizard-hunters,
arm-punchers, lunch-nabbers.
All our games were fair as oceans,
rivers, indefatigable and steady, mapped
and plotted on a grid of our own making.
I played and won. None of us knew better.

Late one summer,
I touched a downy upper lip—
ran my thumb over its edge like a seal,
feeling the prickle of the words
we'd no longer be allowed to speak.
That first long fall
those alien, distrustful years
the planet changed
into a solid winter.

Or so it seemed.
Beneath the skin,
an even wider river ran:
woman, man.
I learned to listen to its silent course,

and lay asleep, ashore.
Those first few sails—
the old maps failed, and we fell,
and there were dragons there.
We tamed them all,
gave them names: Lust was fiercest,
an incorrigible scorcher; Love was gentle,
quiet, easily broken.

Suddenly the old fathers became visible,
sat down long enough to speak to,
some of them worn out by the washing
into flattened disks of soap
and just as useful. There is no comfort
I can bring. No dry newspaper.
No absent talk of baseball.
Then there are the mariners,
claw-grasped, urgent-eyed
as fortune tellers. Their whole bodies
arced like questions.
All the stories must be told,
the work that clanged their bones
in the concave body bell
now still. I bend to listen to the echo,
ever fainter, and sate their need to tell.
I listen well.

The young ones lost to the long winter
are lost still, wrapped up in their skins
like snow dwellers.
They see me sideways, suspiciously;
they think I'm full of secrets.
I never was.

Ode to the Letter W

You're not the mysterious X,
or the brave A, first in all activities,
bane of the shy. You're not even
the confident B, who without
excelling makes a superior effort
and knows—here you are
compatriots—how to follow.

Though you're rare as a K
you are never silent, and in fact
have made the H and N
your bitches. You'll get that R yet—
don't wring your hands over it.
I can hear you in all my wrongs,
in the wren's twitter, in the wrinkle
in my wrap. I can hear you. You are
basic, W, you help me with my
whos, whats, whens, wheres, and whys.
Who cares about how? It doesn't
matter how you get where you want
to be. So what

             if the damned U gets
all the credit, if you're nothing but
redundant, the only double-anything?
It makes you more letter than is
necessary. You are excess—but
in a good way, like a third glass
of wine. Don't think for one moment
as you zigzag through the dictionary
that you are merely functional,
a shortcut on the way to wisdom,
a toothless vowel, or like the Y,

a sometimes consonant. No—
W, you are wicked, baby, wonderful.
You're wheel and winch and wood.
woman, and wife, and word.

ABOUT THE AUTHOR

Celia Lisset Alvarez is a graduate of the University of Miami creative writing program. She is the author of three previous collections of poetry, *Shapeshifting* (winner of the 2005 Spire Press Poetry Award), *The Stones* (Finishing Line Press 2006), and *Multiverses* (Finishing Line Press 2021). Her poetry, stories, essays, and reviews have appeared in numerous journals and anthologies, and she has been nominated for both a Pushcart Prize and a Best of the Net Award. She is currently the editor of *Prospectus: A Literary Offering*. Alvarez was born in Madrid, Spain, to Cuban parents fleeing from Castro's communist regime. The family relocated to Miami, Florida, where she has lived ever since.

www.celialissetalvarez.com

facebook.com/Hobomok
twitter.com/CeliaLisset
instagram.com/hobomok

ALSO BY CELIA LISSET ALVAREZ

Multiverses. Georgetown, KY: Finishing Line Press 2021

Shapeshifting. NY: Spire Press 2006

The Stones. Georgetown, KY: Finishing Line Press 2006

www.ingramcontent.com/pod-product-compliance
Lightning Source LLC
Chambersburg PA
CBHW031448120626

46545CB00006B/2611